HANNAH BELANSZKY is a writer, actor and Yuwaalaraay woman based in Sydney. She is the recipient of the 2025 Balnaves Fellowship with Belvoir St Theatre, which has long been recognised as one of the most prestigious playwriting awards in Australia. Her debut mainstage play *don't ask what the bird look like* (2023) premiered at Queensland Theatre, was shortlisted for the Nick Enright Prize for Playwriting, and was a finalist for the Queensland Premier's Drama Award as well as the Lord Mayor's Award for Best New Australian Work. Her play *Saplings* (2024) premiered at Australian Theatre for Young People as part of Sydney Festival and will have a national tour including the Sydney Opera House in 2026. Hannah wrote, directed and performed in *The Wives of Wolfgang* (2017), which won Best Cabaret at the Adelaide Fringe weekly awards and has also been performed at Fringe World Perth and Brisbane Powerhouse. Hannah has also been in writers' rooms for Jungle Entertainment, Matchbox Pictures, See-Saw Films, Bunya Productions and New Canvas. She has also worked as a Development Coordinator for Unless Pictures, and was selected for the 2022 Netflix ANZ Writer's Journey Lab in partnership with Australians in Film.

Hannah is currently working on a number of projects, including 2025 commissions for Griffin Theatre Company, Queensland Theatre, and Australian Theatre for Young People (ATYP).

Saplings

BY Hannah Belanszky

CURRENT THEATRE SERIES

First published in 2025
by Currency Press Pty Ltd,
Gadigal Land, Suite 310, 46–56 Kippax Street, Surry Hills, NSW 2010, Australia
enquiries@currency.com.au
www.currency.com.au

in association with ATYP

Typeset by Brighton Gray for Currency Press.
Printed by Fineline Print + Copy Services, Revesby, NSW.
Cover shows Maliyan Blair and Ioane Sa'ula.
Cover design by Melanie Raveendran for ATYP.

Currency Press acknowledges the Traditional Owners of the Country on which we live and work. We pay our respects to all Aboriginal and Torres Strait Islander Elders, past and present.

A catalogue record for this book is available from the National Library of Australia

Contents

Playwright's Note

Saplings has been unlike any project I've worked on before.

Over the course of a year, George Kemp (ATYP), Veronica Gordon (Youth Action) and myself spoke with young people from Marrickville to Moree about their various interactions with the law. This included young people involved with the police, who've been to court, are currently incarcerated or recently released. The intention was to create a work of fictional stories based off real conversations with young people involved in our justice system right now.

All I can say is, when I attended the very first workshop early in 2023 at Midjuburi Youth Centre in Marrickville, I had no idea just how much these young people and their stories would work their way into my heart. I also had no idea how much table tennis we'd need to play (I'm uncoordinated), but it was through play that a lot of our best conversations happened. Really, all these young people want is someone to hang out with and listen.

The young people I met were charming, funny and sincere. They aren't victims. They make mistakes. Friendship and loyalty are everything to them. From the outset, it was actually hard to imagine some of them in conflict with the law, but I soon learnt that behind a great sense of humour, are young people in highly complicated situations even most adults would struggle with. Not only are their lives far from straightforward, but the system they're wound up in isn't either, and there are years of distrust to make up for. It's a perpetual cycle of one thing impacting the other, and in the end, none of it helps the young person who only wants to be a kid.

I don't have the answers to all of this, but I did want you to see what I saw. Our young ones deserve our time, and they need our compassion.

I'd like to thank the youth workers, staff members and organisations who helped facilitate these conversations. I also want to acknowledge Jane FitzGerald and George Kemp for their support as I took on these stories to write a play, as well as the incredible actors and creatives I worked with from development through to the premiere production.

I especially want to thank all the young people I spoke to for their bravery in entrusting me with their stories. This play is for them.

Hannah Belanszky

… (truncated)

ATYP Acknowledgements

ATYP would like to acknowledge that we are a company that works and creates on the traditional lands and waters of the Gadigal people, and we are grateful to be telling stories on First Nations country that has such a rich history of storytelling. We pay our respects to Elders past and present.

ATYP worked with Youth Action NSW, the peak body for organisations working in Youth Justice in NSW, to develop a performance that would communicate the lived experience of young people in contact with the justice system. The aim of the project was to develop a theatre production from a series of workshops involving young people with lived experience with the justice system from Western Sydney and Regional NSW.

These workshops were held on the lands of the Kamilaroi, Gadigal and Wangal, Gundungurra and Dharug, and Dharawal peoples.

ATYP would like to thank:

Andrew Johnson—Thrive International
Youth Action NSW
Kate Munro
Veronica Gordon
Midjuburi Youth Resource Centre
Miyay Birray Youth Services
Darrel Smith
Youth Off The Streets
Street University Katoomba
Reiby Youth Justice Centre
Sydney Festival
Hal Cumpston
Chelsea Hawke
Solomon Holder
Aaron McGrath

NSW Government—Department of Communities and Justice
NSW Government—Create NSW
NSW Government—Office for Regional Youth

Saplings was first presented by Australian Theatre for Young People and Youth Action as part of the 2024 Sydney Festival, from 25 January to 4 February 2024 at the Rebel Theatre, ATYP, Eora Country.

The cast was as follows:

Maliyan Blair
Nyasha Ogden
Wesley Patten
Ioane Sa'ula
Anthony Yangoyan (understudy)

Writer, Hannah Belanszky
Director, Abbie-lee Lewis
Dramaturg, Jane FitzGerald
Co-Set and Costume Designer, Angela Doherty
Co-Set and Lighting Designer, Morgan Moroney
Composer & Sound Designer, Michael Weir
Associate Sound Designer, Gryffyn Long
Fight Director, Tim Dashwood
Production Manager, Harry Dowling
Stage Manager, Milly Grindrod
Producer, Hayden Tonazzi
Workshop Facilitator, George Kemp

CHARACTERS

Scene 1 – The Reserve

KAI, male, First Nations.

JONTY, male, First Nations.

Scene 2 – Stolen Watch

YANI, male.

LEO, male.

MARA, female.

Scene 3 – Mi Goreng Interrogation

LACHY, male.

Scene 4 – The Courthouse

ALINTA, female.

SANDON, male.

Scene 5 – Juvie

RYAN, male.

BILLY, male.

SAL, male.

Scene 6 – Train Station

SHANIKA, female.

ISAIAH, male.

Scene 7 – Photography

JADE, female.

Scene 8 – Birthday Cake

JARRAH, male.

ASH, male.

NIKKI, female.

DARIUS, male.

Scene 9 – Bail Bed

CORBAN, male.

Scene 10 – Community Garden

KAI, male, First Nations (same as Scene 1).

JONTY, male, First Nations (same as Scene 1).

CASTING

This play is for a cast of four actors:

1 female (First Nations)
2 male (First Nations)
1 male (non-Indigenous)

The actors should have a playing age range of approximately 13–18.

SCENE 1: THE RESERVE

Night-time on the Reserve.

JONTY *and* KAI *are taking turns excitedly jumping over a small campfire in Kai's yard.*

JONTY: You go, you go

KAI *braces himself in a runner's position. He takes a run at the fire and jumps. They both yell.*

KAI: WOOOOOOO!
JONTY: WOOOOOOO!

KAI *lands on the other side, exhilarated.*

That was your best one!
KAI: Think I burnt my foot a bit
JONTY: Okay, my turn

JONTY *runs at the fire and jumps over.*

Damn. Still can't get as high as you
KAI: Nah you got some good air
JONTY: I got higher before
KAI: Start further back. Get a run up

JONTY *lines up, further back this time.*

JONTY: Wait, what if we … ?

They look at each other and grin. They've had the same idea.

KAI: Same time?
JONTY: Same time?

KAI *lines up.*

KAI: Alright. Three, two—

They are both about to run when they look over in the direction of the house. Kai's mum is calling out to them. They remain frozen in this position.

[*Yelling out*] What?
Nothing. We're not doing anything
Okay. See ya tomorrow

JONTY: See ya!
KAI: Yeah, we'll go to bed

She leaves. Their attention returns to the fire. The exhilaration has quickly disappeared.

JONTY: Dunno if I can make that again
KAI: Yeah, my foot still kinda hurts

They sit down beside the fire.

So what now?
JONTY: Where's your mum going so late?
KAI: She's working at the old-person centre
JONTY: That's so far
KAI: She starts really early on Thursdays so she's gotta leave now. Wish there was something on tonight
JONTY: She still talking 'bout moving towns?
KAI: I think some people are at the creek. Should we head?

JONTY *shakes his head, disinterested.*

What about the park? We could go to the park
JONTY: Ehhh
KAI: Servo?
JONTY: Nah
KAI: Servo — but we get extra lollies?

Pause.

JONTY: Nah
KAI: We could go to the sign for a bit. Try catch a ride
JONTY: We did that last night
KAI: You think of something
JONTY: I dunno
KAI: We could moon the trucks? Remember that time we mooned the trucks?

Pause.

Okay, let's go to your house
JONTY: Nah, not mine
KAI: I don't wanna stay home all night
JONTY: Your house is better

KAI: It's a Reserve house. They're the same
JONTY: Yeah but mine's boring. Really boring
KAI: Come on
JONTY: We can't
KAI: My house is boring too. And the fire's getting shit now anyway
JONTY: There's no power at my place. We got cut off
KAI: Oh

Pause.

Is it gonna get put back on?
JONTY: Dunno. No-one's there. It's all dark
KAI: We could watch scary movies in the dark! That could be cool!
JONTY: You need power to watch TV
KAI: Oh yeah. Alright, we can stay here

They sit. Bored.

JONTY: I know what we could do

He looks at KAI, *who knows exactly what he's suggesting.*

KAI: Not this again
JONTY: Aw, come on
KAI: I told you, it's not my thing
JONTY: Let me pitch it to you one more time
KAI: No
JONTY: Yeah, imma pitch it one more time
KAI: Ehhh
JONTY: Kai and Jonty: Music Duo

Pause.

KAI: Bro that sounds lamer than the first hundred times you said it
JONTY: It's just the concept. You know, the vision?
KAI: I could never
JONTY: Two brothers on the Reserve making music together
KAI: People would laugh
JONTY: No, they wouldn't. Not if we were good. Not if we got famous
KAI: How can we get famous if we can't even sing?
JONTY: Speak for yourself
KAI: Can't write a song either

JONTY: Yes, I can
KAI: No-one from out here gets famous anyway
JONTY: We would. And I've heard you sing before
KAI: When?
JONTY: You thought I was taking a nap
KAI: What!
JONTY: Yeah

Pause.

KAI: So … what … . did you … think?
JONTY: Not bad
KAI: Really?
JONTY: Pretty good, actually. That's how I got the idea
KAI: [*flattered*] No
JONTY: Yeah
KAI: Sometimes I think maybe I can sing a little bit. But only if it's the right song
JONTY: It'll always be the right song if it's ours. And it wouldn't be that hard either. I've heard of so many people who started out making music at home
KAI: Yeah, but they had connections
JONTY: All they did was post their songs online, and people listened to them and liked them and then they got so much money. We could buy new shoes …
KAI: I want Nikes
JONTY: A new house …
KAI: One near the park?
JONTY: And we wouldn't need to go to school anymore
KAI: You don't go anyway
JONTY: Yeah, 'cause I been busy writing these lyrics brah
KAI: Really?
JONTY: Not yet, but I been thinking about it
KAI: So what's the song gonna be?
JONTY: Anything. Whatever we wanna say
KAI: That'd be cool
JONTY: It'll be more fun than the creek. Better than the servo, or mooning trucks

KAI: Still kinda embarrassing

JONTY: It's only embarrassing if I do it alone. I can't be in a duo by myself. I'm no solo artist. It has to be the two of us or it doesn't work

KAI *thinks.*

Please, brother, please, I kind of—Never mind

KAI: What?

JONTY: Let's go to the servo

KAI: What were you gonna say?

JONTY: It's stupid

KAI: I won't be in the duo if you don't tell me

JONTY *is suddenly all shy.*

JONTY: I just … I thought if we did this then maybe—I kinda wanna pay the power bill for Mum one day, alright

KAI *caves.*

KAI: I really hope I can sing as good as you think

JONTY: Is that … ? Do you mean … ?

KAI: Maybe

JONTY: YES!

KAI: Shhhh

JONTY: What? You scared everyone on the Reserve is gonna hear that KAI IS A MUSIC MAKER? SINGER AND A SHAKER? MASTER OF THE BEATS?

KAI: Shut the fuck up

JONTY: Better get used to it, brother!

KAI: I think we keep it quiet

JONTY: What!

KAI: Until we actually make something first

JONTY: Ehhh

KAI: Then it's like a surprise

JONTY: Okay, yeah, I'm down with that

KAI: But like, how do we make a song?

JONTY: Oh, easy. On this special app. You can voice record, add a beat

KAI: Damn

JONTY: Nah, it's legit

KAI: We can't do that

JONTY: It's what a lot of the artists do, trust me
KAI: But you lost your phone
JONTY: You've got one

KAI *looks sheepish.*

Don't you?

KAI *pulls out an old iPhone with an extremely smashed screen.*

The fuck. Your phone is proper shit
KAI: It fell outta my pocket climbing out that window, remember
JONTY: Oh, yeah

JONTY *inspects the phone.*

We can still work with this
KAI: No, we can't
JONTY: We'll figure it out
KAI: You can't read anything. If my texts are fucked, the song'll be even worse
JONTY: But we can't give up now. I just finally changed your mind. All we need is a phone, with a screen, and then we can basically do anything, we could be the next big thing
KAI: We don't have money for a new one. Sorry, Jonty

Pause.

JONTY: I'm going home
KAI: You can't go home, you've got no lights
JONTY: I'm just gonna sleep anyway

He begins to leave.

KAI: Jonty

JONTY *doesn't turn back.*

There's a lot of people watching the horse hockey tonight. There'd be a few empty houses

JONTY *turns around. They look at each other. They've both had the same thought.*

JONTY: We said we weren't gonna do that again
KAI: We don't have to burn this one down. We could be in and out, real quick

JONTY: Get some cash
KAI: Buy a new phone
JONTY: And make some music!

They do their special handshake.

Deal
KAI: Deal

They start leaving together, both excited.

JONTY: You know what this means, right? We need stage names, brother!

SCENE 2: STOLEN WATCH

Just after midnight.

LEO, YANI *and* MARA *sneak back into Leo's house. They are lit by phone torches as they enter. They'll pass a vape between themselves throughout.*

LEO: Shh! You'll wake her up
YANI: Geez you're more scared of your nan than the cops

LEO *turns on a light. He starts emptying out his backpack. A few notes of cash. Not a lot.*

Bro you said they were loaded
LEO: Would've been more in that side room
YANI: Nah there was nothing there
LEO: And they are loaded, you saw the place
MARA: That house was so white
YANI: Creepy
MARA: Too white
LEO: What about youse?

YANI *tosses some AirPods at him.*

YANI: We should've hit up the one next door
LEO: Nah they've got cameras
MARA: What about that one across the road with the stone walls and the archway?
LEO: Fuck no. I work at that house

YANI: He helped build the archway

LEO: I'm telling you, there would've been more in the side room

MARA: I swear the lady in there saw us

LEO: She was asleep

YANI: People usually sleep upstairs, not down

LEO: It was too dark anyway

YANI: And usually they have cash just lyin' around, everywhere, all over the place. If Tyson was there, he'd find it

Pause.

LEO: [*to* MARA] Get anything good?

MARA: Dunno

She pulls out a watch. They are impressed.

YANI: Fuck that's—what's that?

LEO *inspects the watch.*

LEO: Omega

YANI: Omega! These go for like twenty K

LEO: More

MARA: It was in the kitchen

LEO: Of course these people have twenty K sitting in the kitchen. They don't even care. They don't even need it

YANI: Glad we brought you, Mara

MARA: So how—What do we do with it?

YANI: Leo can take it to—

LEO: Nah, I can't this time

YANI: Aw, come on

LEO: I'm on house arrest, bro

YANI: You still go out

LEO: Only 'cause it got amended for school or my apprenticeship but that's it. That's all I can do

YANI: Yeah, so take it on your way home tomorrow

LEO: I don't want it on me

YANI: Leo

LEO: Yani

YANI: You came out with us tonight

LEO: Why can't you do it?

YANI: You're less likely to get stopped than me. They stop me, like, literally search me, almost every time I'm on the street. Can't catch me though. Except for this one time I got done, but that was different

LEO: It was your asthma

YANI: [*motioning to the vape*] Gimme

LEO *passes it over.*

Nah, that copper was fast. He said he used to play soccer or some shit

LEO: It was your fuckin asthma

YANI: [*To* MARA] This was before you came to our school. Basically, I gassed this cop up the hill—Tyson was there too, and Tyson goes to the copper, 'You can't catch us, you're fat.' Anyway, it's a big fucking hill, so I stop for like a second

LEO: Asthma

YANI: And I look back and the copper's right there. He jumps on me, fully squashes me, and he's like, your mate said I wouldn't catch you, but look, look what happened, I had to catch you, to show your friend I'm not too slow. Then he took me in, took me to the cells. I was there all night

MARA: I'd just sleep

LEO: You can't do that anymore

MARA: They don't let you?

LEO: If you sleep then they can't question you or some shit. They can keep you for six hours but if you sleep, that time gets extended, like the six hours don't count

YANI: If you can sneak your vape in, it's alright

LEO: Or your phone. I'll show you my trick

YANI: Nah I'll show her

LEO: You don't even do it

YANI: Yes I do. And it's Tyson's trick, not yours

LEO: Okay so, when they take you in, they make you do this body scanner thing, but the trick is to ask for a body *search* instead. So then they strip you and you gotta take everything off, but you don't want them to see, like, *everything*, so you stand like this—

He puts his hands in front of his privates.

—but you just hold your vape in your hand the whole time while they search you

YANI: If I've got my vape in there with me, I'm sweet
LEO: Dunno how that works for girls, though
MARA: It would still work the same
LEO: Would it?

Pause.

YANI: Anyway, all I did that night was break curfew, but that copper wanted to prove he was a track star, otherwise usually I'm faster than the cops. Way faster
LEO: Yeah, yeah
MARA: Okay so Leo's taking the watch?
YANI: [*at the same time*] Yes
LEO: [*at the same time*] No
YANI: Come on, do it for me, brother. [*Motioning towards* MARA] I need this
LEO: Why?
YANI: 'Cause I only just got off bail today. I haven't been to the Easter Show in three years, not since I was ten, 'cause I've been on bail every time it's on. I really wanna go this year
LEO: I can't go either
YANI: [*to* MARA] You're going to the show, right?
MARA: Should I?
YANI: You just moved here. You gotta go
MARA: Okay
YANI: Go on Saturday, that's when I'm going
LEO: Get me the sour worms bag, I love sour worms
YANI: I'll get you every bag if you take the fuckin watch. Like I seriously can't get searched with that watch on me. It's my first day being free
LEO: Bail takes forever
YANI: Exactly! So take the watch take the watch take the watch for me
LEO: That's why I kinda wanted to take the charge this time, to not have to be on bail again. I'm over this. Every time I'm on house arrest, I gotta stay here at Nan's
YANI: Yeah but if you take the charge you could get locked up and you don't want that. Actually, someone told me once there's this thing you can plead where you can get out of things
MARA: Really?

LEO: In my dreams
YANI: Yeah, it's called … Doli?
LEO: Doli
YANI: Yeah, Doli something. I can't remember
MARA: What's it mean?
YANI: I dunno, I think it's like, if you get caught you plead Doli and it means you're a kid and you didn't know you were wrong
LEO: That wouldn't work
YANI: Apparently till you're fourteen
LEO: Okay so, Doli Something
YANI: No it's not fucking Doli Something it's—okay, it's Doli Inca … Doli Incapax. I think that's it
MARA: Doli Incapax
LEO: So if we get caught tonight
MARA: Will we? I still think that lady downstairs was awake
LEO: Well if she was, you can try it
MARA: So I say I didn't know
YANI: Yeah, you're just a kid
LEO: You're not a criminal

Pause.

YANI: Just take the Omega, so we can get that sweet money. I wanna get the electric scooter already. That's the dream, Leo
LEO: The dream
YANI: The dream

Pause.

LEO: Sorry, Yani
YANI: Come on!
LEO: I don't want my house arrest extended. I'm going crazy here. Nan's been teaching me to crochet a blanket
YANI: But if we buy the scooter we can keep it
LEO: So you take it then
YANI: I'm not missing the show
MARA: I'll take the watch. Where do I go?

LEO *and* YANI *look at* MARA, *then each other, and laugh.* MARA *is embarrassed.*

What?

LEO: Nothing

MARA: No, what?

YANI: That watch is worth dollar bills, baby girl

LEO: So we gotta sell it, we're not gonna wear it or nothing

YANI: Do you even know what we could get?

MARA: I'm the one who found it

YANI: You gotta know how to—You couldn't handle it

MARA: Why not?

YANI: You're too …

LEO: She's too …

YANI: Yeah it's like, cop walks past, looks at her once, and she sweats and she goes, here sir, here, found this watch here, look

LEO: Ha!

MARA: I will not

LEO: They'll ask you where you got it, it'll be reported stolen already

YANI: You can say you found it wherever, but they'll still take you in for questioning

LEO: Ask where you were, who your friends are

YANI: They'll find out you were with me

LEO: And me. You probably won't get charged since you handed it in, especially since it's your first time, but we'll lose the watch

YANI: And then they'll bring us in, here we go again, back on bail, curfew

LEO: House arrest

YANI: Bye bye scooter. And we need that scooter

MARA: But I won't hand it in. I won't say anything

LEO: It's an even split. Always. You'll still get the money

MARA: I'm not scared of the cops, okay. They're fucking dumb

YANI: Aye!

MARA: I can walk past them, no problem. I've done it before at my old school. I was at the park with my friend and her older brother. They were drinking and smoking—just yandi, then the cops rolled up. My friends split—They ran off and jumped in the bushes, but they forgot to take the yandi, like they just left it on the table! So I put it in my bag, real calm. Cops walked by, they had no idea

LEO: Ooooh

MARA: My friends were trying so hard not to laugh in the bushes

YANI: Cops are gronks

LEO: That youth liaison officer, what's his face, he's alright sometimes, isn't he?

YANI: They're good when the body cams are on. Oh, you want something to eat, you wanna cuppa tea? Turn the camera off, never come back—you just sit there for hours in your cell, starving, no-one talks to you. And when they see you on the street, like, if they found that Omega watch on me, they find anything on me—they just push you up against the wall, the fence, maybe bash ya, maybe even take whatever you got for themselves. Nah. If they're not gonna respect me, I'm not gonna respect them. Especially after what they did to Tyson

Pause.

LEO: Can't believe it's been a year

YANI: Feels like a year when you're thinking 'bout it all the time

MARA: I saw it on TV back home

YANI: See that Porsche me and Tyson drove? It was a four-wheel-drive, you know the ones

LEO: Real smooth

YANI: Leather seats, sunroof, tinted windows. Beautiful. I hooked up my phone, played music, we were just cruising, you know. Ever driven a Porsche?

MARA: I've never driven a car

LEO: They're fast

YANI: Real fast. But Tyson had to speed up even more 'cause the cops found us and they were going fast, so it was like—well, Tyson had to go fast too, or they'd catch us. The engine on that car, man, it was like, I dunno, it kinda lurched or something and then this pole, fuck I dunno where that pole came from

Pause.

MARA: Tragic accident, they said

YANI: It wasn't an accident. It was a race, and they wanted to win

MARA: So shit

Pause.

I'm not gonna freak about the cops or anything. I can take the watch and I can get the money. Let me do it

YANI *and* LEO *look at each other.*

YANI: Once you get your first arrest, once they know your face, your name—you can't go anywhere, you can't do nothing

LEO: They'll always watch you

YANI: No second chances

Pause.

MARA: Give it to me

They hand her the watch.

YANI: Fuck yeah, I'm gonna be so fast on that scooter

LEO: We should get two

YANI: Three! I'll race ya

MARA: Yew!

Sounds of movement outside on the street. They're all instantly on edge.

You hear that?

They listen.

YANI: Is that your nan?

LEO: I think they're outside

YANI: Quick, pretend you're asleep

LEO *turns off the lights.*

They hear footsteps coming closer.

They wait, in suspense.

A loud knock on the door.

LEO: Fuck!

YANI: How'd they find us already?

MARA: I told you that woman saw us

Another knock.

What do we do?

LEO: You can't be here, they'll find out I broke bail

YANI: They already know

The knocking continues.

MARA: Do we run? What do we—

YANI: Fuck it
MARA: Yani!
YANI: Not doing this again

> YANI *climbs out the window and starts running. The police see him and start chasing him away from the house.*
>
> MARA *and* LEO *are left behind. They look at each other, then to the police.*

MARA: Doli? Doli Incapax?

SCENE 3: MI GORENG INTERROGATION

LACHY *has just been brought into the police station.*

LACHY: I wasn't there 'cause I wanted to be, I was there 'cause I had to be, okay? Nowhere else was open and I thought I could just go in and go out and no-one would notice. This is all 'cause of Josh. If Josh hadn't eaten my noodles, I wouldn't be here.

Josh, yeah, that's my stepbrother.

Well, there was only one packet left in the whole house and he knew they were mine, he knew not to touch them. I've been working on my patience lately but this whole day has—it's really—it's really making it hard for me.

I didn't get much sleep either. While I'm on twenty-four-hour curfew and can't leave the house, I've been up watching every movie The Rock has ever made. *Red Notice*, *G.I. Joe*, *Fast and Furious Six*, *Furious Seven* … I just like him, I like action, you know.

I'd only been asleep two hours when I woke up, 'cause—I don't know what they were fighting about, but they never close the door. It's annoying. They wake me up all the time. They wake up Josh, too. Even the neighbours, they wake up the neighbours—ask Susie next door, she hates us. Anyway, I'm one of those people, once I wake up, it's hard to go back to sleep. So I'm just lying there, and—you know when you wake up and your bladder is really full, but you don't wanna get out of bed? So you try and ignore it so you can stay under the blanket, but it's not going away, and you know you won't be able to go back to sleep, won't be able to do anything else, not until you pee? Yeah, it was kinda like that. Need to pee but can't. Except for me, I couldn't pee 'cause I'm not allowed out of my room.

It's not that I can't come out ever, but I've got to be careful when I do, 'cause of the in-house AVO Josh has against me. I know if he reports me, you'll say I've broke bail, so I've been really good with that. I don't touch any of his stuff, I don't talk to him, I'm never, ever, in the same room—and that's not easy, okay, our house isn't big or anything.

Usually what I do is I put my ear on the wall 'cause he's got the room next to mine, so I check that he's in there before I come out. But today they were just so loud, like I'm not kidding, I was listening at the wall but I couldn't hear anything, couldn't hear anything else, and so I start pacing. I'm just pacing and holding this pee in while they're going off, I mean, I still don't know what they were going off about but they were going on and on and on and I didn't know what else to do, I was either going to pee in a Coke bottle or pee my pants 'cause I was not going out there, no, I was not leaving my room, but then SLAM!

Dunno where they went, just out the front door. Car's gone, so. Dunno.

But then I could finally hear Josh in his room, so, coast clear, I went, did my business.

You ever played FIFA? PS5? The latest one just came out. I downloaded last night. I play online with my friends—I haven't seen them in ages except for on Snapchat and we've been waiting forever for this release. Oh, and I've got the best set-up. Yeah, it's kinda like, bed here, TV there, and then I've my chair here, so I can put my feet up on the bed—it's the perfect view, perfectly comfortable …

When I came back from the toilet, I could tell. Josh had been in my room. He does things like this—when we had all those fights, it wasn't just me, okay, it was him too, and now he wants an excuse to report me for breaching the AVO. But I told you, I been working on my patience lately, I really have.

But this … This got me. So my game was downloaded, right, and my friends, all my friends were online, all messaging me about it, and I had to tell them I couldn't play, I couldn't even load the game, you know why? Josh! He took my controller! I dunno where he's put it. Ask him. It's probably in his room somewhere. Or broken. But it didn't matter 'cause I couldn't ask my dad to ask Josh's mum to get it from Josh 'cause they were gone somewhere and I didn't know when they'd be back.

I wanted to go in there myself. Like I—I really wanted to—

I decided to make some Mi Goreng instead. The instant kind in the packets is my favourite thing to eat. The only thing I eat, 'cause it's quick. I can sneak into the kitchen, make it really fast, then get back to my room without having to talk to anyone. I get a bowl from the sink, put the jug on—imagining kicking back with a big bowl of noodles and watching The Rock in *Snitch*—I hear it's a pretty good movie. But I couldn't find the Mi Goreng anywhere. I looked properly and everything. I know I had one packet left, I was saving it for today and I always put it in the same spot.

And then I saw it. A red packet, on the floor. EMPTY.

I was standing there with the empty packet when Josh walks out of his room with an EMPTY BOWL.

I know I'm not supposed to talk to him but okay, I did. But it just came out and all I said was,

Those were my noodles!

He looks at me, goes,

What else am I 'sposed to eat?

So then I go through the fridge and I open all the cupboards and all the drawers and he's right, there's nothing in there, just empty packets, empty boxes, empty cans, and I'm suddenly so hungry and so angry and I can't believe he ate my noodles and I can't believe no-one bought more noodles and I can't believe I'm stuck in this house when I can't eat anything or talk to anyone and I can't play PlayStation either.

So then I just—okay, this is the part you're not gonna like.

I found thirteen dollars and I went outside.

The sun. On my face.

But I had a mission, okay. I wasn't breaking my curfew to do anything but go to the corner store and come straight back.

I was walking there thinking 'bout what I was gonna buy, 'cause I realised with thirteen dollars, I could get more than noodles, I could get ice-cream too. But when I got there, I remembered. It's Sunday.

Okay so, I know I wasn't supposed to talk to Josh, and I know I wasn't supposed to leave the house, but the next part isn't all my fault, it's this town's fault for having everything except Woolworths shut on a Sunday.

I've had the lifetime ban at every Woolies in Australia since I was twelve for stealing, but I haven't been there in ages. And I wasn't gonna be stealing this time either, 'cause I had thirteen dollars. And also, I've gotten taller lately, I really didn't think they'd recognise me.

Still, I walked real sneaky, head down, straight into Woolies. But then I remembered how if you look sneaky, people notice you more, so I stand up real straight, you know, act normal. I walk normal to the noodle aisle. Walk normal to the freezer. And then I walk normal to the front of the store and I'm just so happy no-one has called the cops on me and I've got Mi Goreng and a whole box of Maxibons.

Self-serve was closed so I had to go the checkout.

I put the food down on the counter.

I was still trying to act normal, but the checkout lady, I dunno, she seemed kinda nice, she kept smiling at me.

I give her the money.

She gives me the receipt.

I walk out of the store, and …

I kept thinking, if I get away with this, I might let Josh have one of these Maxibons.

They're probably melted now. But what about the noodles?

Do you have my noodles?

SCENE 4: THE COURTHOUSE

ALINTA *and* SANDON *are waiting at the children's courts.*

ALINTA *barely looks up from her phone. Sounds of TikTok videos as she scrolls.*

SANDON *looks around, bright-eyed, restless.*

SANDON: So … we just … sit here

ALINTA: Mmhmm

SANDON: All day

ALINTA: Uh-huh

SANDON: We sit here. All day. And wait

ALINTA: Yep

Beat.

SANDON: BORING

ALINTA: Told you

SANDON: No, you didn't. No-one ever told me that court is the most boring place on Earth

ALINTA: They probably did, but you weren't listening

SANDON: Well, clearly the stuff on TV is false advertising. I thought there was gonna be some real hectic shit going on. Like all the media swarming, cameras flashing as I walk in. Boss bitches in wigs. A brawl in the foyer. But nah, this place is like, worse than the line at Centrelink and I didn't even bring a phone charger

He looks hopefully at ALINTA.

ALINTA: No

SANDON: I mean, it's still cool we're here. To actually be at court means it's real now. Which is obviously, like, pretty sick

ALINTA *keeps scrolling.*

Do you know where the toilet is?

ALINTA: Didn't you just go?

SANDON: Well, yeah, but

ALINTA: Nervous pee?

SANDON: No

ALINTA: Nervous poo?

SANDON: No! I'm not nervous. I just thought there might be another toilet to try, you know, for fun?

ALINTA: Just the one …

SANDON: Damn. There's not even any food either

ALINTA: I pack my own

SANDON: At least I know someone here

ALINTA: Yeah, it's usually just randoms. Until you see someone you know

SANDON: And I've got Ted. The man. I love how you can literally ring Ted up any time and he'll be there. He came and got me from the station, gives me money. Now he's come to court with me and everything

ALINTA: Everyone loves Ted

SANDON: Except my dad

ALINTA: At least your dad is here. Mum's had too much time off work. They put every single charge on a different day, so you have to keep coming back

SANDON: Hold up. You have to come back?

ALINTA: Yeah?

SANDON: You have to come back and sit here and do all this, all over again?

ALINTA: And again, and again

SANDON: How?!

ALINTA: Well, you walk in using your legs and sit in a chair using your bum and then you shut up about it

SANDON: Nup, couldn't do that

ALINTA: You're gonna have to, if your lawyer doesn't show

SANDON: Ted said she'll get here eventually. He just rang her again

ALINTA: They say they're on their way but sometimes they're busy and they flake

SANDON: What happens then?

ALINTA: You reschedule

SANDON: Reschedule?!

ALINTA: Yep

SANDON: But I can't reschedule, that's not an option for me

ALINTA: No-one cares

SANDON: But that's not fair. I'm here now

ALINTA: So?

SANDON: So, she has to show up. I'm already going insane from all this waiting. I might have to start some drama myself. I'm deteriorating

ALINTA: You've been here ten minutes

SANDON: It's been longer than that

He checks the time. She's right. He lets out a huge dramatic wail and slumps back into his chair.

Ahhhhhhh

ALINTA: You done?

SANDON: Not really

ALINTA: Great

They keep sitting, waiting, scrolling.

SANDON: But I assume once I get in there, that's when shit really hits the fan. You know, like, when I take to the stand and everything pops off?

ALINTA: It only takes five minutes

SANDON: To what? Say my piece?

ALINTA: The whole thing. And what piece? I wouldn't know what to say even if they gave me the chance

SANDON: So that's it? The whole hearing? Five minutes. All this day waiting for five minutes?

ALINTA: It's just some old guy lecturing you

SANDON: So, basically my life up to this point

ALINTA: And they only talk to the lawyer. You don't get to say anything, apart from when you say, I understand, or thank you, or some shit. And the whole time, everyone in the room is staring at you

SANDON: So they're all gonna look at me? I can work with that

ALINTA: It's actually kinda fucked up

Pause.

SANDON: But you still have to know what to plead, right? That's the big finale

ALINTA: Yeah, guilty or not guilty

SANDON: And so do you decide that beforehand or do you feel it in the moment

ALINTA: Your lawyer should've already told you what to plead

SANDON: Well, yeah, but do you do what they say

ALINTA: If you trust them

SANDON: Cool

Pause.

Wait—I shouldn't trust them?

ALINTA: I don't wanna freak you out

SANDON: I won't freak out. Yes, it's my first time at court, but it's not my first time getting in trouble. I've been to a youth justice conference. I've just never reached this level before. Kind of a big deal

ALINTA: It's not a game

SANDON: And yeah, maybe I am kind of confused, but that's only because I've been hearing a lot of … conflicting opinions, and I've got nothing else to do but sit here and think about them for an increasingly obscene length of time, and I don't like thinking about these things, I don't like thinking about anything if I can help it

ALINTA: Now you're talking

SANDON: But you—You seem like you know what you're doing

ALINTA: Nah

SANDON: Yeah, Ted said you …

ALINTA: Ted said what?

SANDON *doesn't reply.*

So this is all because your dad doesn't like Ted

SANDON: Yeah, Dad doesn't like Ted or my lawyer, and my lawyer doesn't like my dad, or Ted. Ted doesn't really like my lawyer either, but he says we should still listen to her and not my dad. And me, I wanna listen to my dad, because he's my dad, but I also wanna listen to Ted, because he's Ted, but also right now Ted is saying we should listen to my lawyer and I don't really buy that, not when she hasn't shown up yet and I don't even get what she's saying half the time. And this is all because my lawyer thinks I should plead not guilty and Dad thinks I should plead guilty because he feels shame about my charges and … And because he says I am. Guilty

ALINTA: That sucks

SANDON: Yeah, he thinks it'll look more favourable if I own up to it. For him or for me, I don't know

Pause.

SANDON: So that's it?

ALINTA: What?

SANDON: Some help you are

ALINTA: I'm stuck here too

SANDON: I thought maybe you knew what to do

ALINTA: How can I? It changes all the time. Different rules, different words. Sometimes it just depends who you get, what mood they're in, if they like your lawyer, if your lawyer likes you, if your lawyer even knows what they're doing or cares what they're doing or even has time

SANDON: That made things much clearer for me, thank you

ALINTA: What do you want me to say?

SANDON: I just thought you might have something more helpful than 'that sucks'

ALINTA: Well, it does suck. The whole thing sucks. Court is nothing like TV until it's exactly like TV. And then that's not even a good thing because it probably means it didn't work out the way you want. Because that's better television

SANDON: Wow, you're really ruining this for me now

ALINTA: Sorry

SANDON: I just wanted to enjoy my first day at court, but everyone is determined to make me, I don't know, 'face reality'? Dad is probably out there now planning an outfit for his first prison visit, 'As you can see, I couldn't possibly have raised my son to do anything like the charges laid upon our name'

ALINTA: Sometimes you get tricked and there is nothing you can do about it

SANDON: I guess my life is over then

ALINTA: I guess you're really annoying then

SANDON: No-one can save me now

ALINTA: Just plead not guilty and you'll be fine

SANDON: Really?

ALINTA: No

SANDON: Then what do I plead?!

ALINTA: I can't help you. I can't control it. I don't even know how it works

SANDON: You really got my hopes up for a second there

ALINTA: All I know is, last time, my lawyer told me to plead guilty and it was the wrong advice. Me and my friend Jesse had the exact same charges, and so much less of a history than Tom—you know Tom? Tom, he was the one who joined our group and got us breaking in and doing all that stuff, like it was his idea in the first place. Anyway, his lawyer told him to plead not guilty and it worked—he got away with it. Charges completely dropped. Even though Tom was also on the video, like you could see his face and ours. But me and Jesse, we pled guilty and got found guilty so now it's on our records and they're gonna know that today when they sentence me for this

SANDON: That actually does suck

ALINTA: Some help you are

SANDON: So do you know what you're pleading today

ALINTA: Yeah

SANDON: That's good, at least

ALINTA: I've got given a different lawyer this time. They seem fine and they listen to me and they're actually here

SANDON: Jealous

ALINTA: But I'm worried that—well, they said my record might work against me

SANDON: What does that mean?

ALINTA: I've had enough warnings

Pause.

So yeah, you never know how it's gonna work out, except that it's gonna drag on and on. So you better get used to it

Pause.

SANDON: If it's any, um—I don't know if it'll make you feel better, and by the way, it's not like we were talking about you or anything—Well, we were, but just a little bit, and only because—Well, because Ted was saying to me that—He said that even though things have been bad for you lately, you've been handling it all like, really well

ALINTA: He said that?

SANDON: Yeah

ALINTA: That's nice

SANDON: Don't rub it in. He said all this good stuff about you, but nothing nice about me. He just told me I need to stop 'carrying on'. Carrying on? I'm not carrying on. Well, maybe a little bit. But how am I supposed to stop?

ALINTA *goes back to scrolling, but* SANDON *can't stay still.*

Well, at least that killed ten minutes.

SCENE 5: JUVIE

Free time outside on the boys' unit at a juvenile justice centre.

BILLY *and* SAL *are passing a ball between them.*

RYAN *storms in.*

BILLY: Hey! Free time's almost up. We been waiting

RYAN: Where is he? Where's the new kid?

BILLY: Why'd you take so long?

RYAN: I knew it was him who's been talking shit under my door. And now, just now, when I was on the phone—

BILLY: [*surprised*] The phone?

RYAN: He got all up in my face, 'cause he knew, he knew I couldn't do anything, not while I was listening, not while I was paying attention to … to the call—Anyway, he came up and had the fucking nerve to flick my cap. That's right, flicked it, just like this, FLICK!

SAL: [*sympathetic to the new kid*] Oh, no …

RYAN: The look on my face, man, no wonder he ran off. So where'd he go? I'm gonna get him! I'm gonna make him BLEED!

SAL: Aw nah, he's alright. He's just new

RYAN: Yeah so someone's gotta teach that little fuck. You can't do that in here. You can't pull that kinda shit with me and get away with it

SAL: Why you swearing so much, bro?

BILLY: You don't wanna get sent your room during free time, not right before lockdown

BILLY *passes* RYAN *the ball.*

Think of the KFC. Hey, Sal?

SAL: Mmmhmm

RYAN: I don't care about KFC

BILLY: [*unspeakable*] What?

RYAN: Not anymore

BILLY: Lies

RYAN: Nup, don't care. Let's go, let's go now, let's get him, Billy

Pause.

BILLY: Ceebs

RYAN: Come on, you're in juvie. Live your life!

BILLY: I've been perfect all week. Chores. Homework. Every single day. Even when I didn't want to

RYAN: Fuck chores. Who cares about KFC?

BILLY *and* SAL *look at each other in shock.*

BILLY / SAL: Us

RYAN: You guys are being gay

SAL: [*serious*] Don't say that

BILLY: I live for the outside food. It's the best feed we get. I'm not risking my Friday night Zinger box. It's the whole reason I'm good

SAL: The boys are always good for chicken

BILLY: And we literally only just got eight-thirty bedtimes. I don't wanna lose that either

SAL *sniggers.*

Yeah, yeah. It's not as good as nine

SAL: Aye

BILLY: But I'm not a suck-up like you

SAL: Hehe

RYAN: Doesn't matter if I eat KFC tonight. Doesn't matter when I go to bed. I just told you. I don't care

SAL *and* BILLY *exchange glances.*

SAL: That don't sound right, bro

BILLY: What's up with you?

RYAN: Nothing

BILLY: Was that your mum on the phone?

RYAN: No

BILLY: Your lawyer?

RYAN: I just wanna kill the new kid for flicking my cap. Why you guys being so lame?

BILLY: Then who were you on the phone to for so long?

SAL: Routines are important. Chicken is important

BILLY: Yeah, and it's our thing

RYAN: Can you both fuck off about the chicken?

SAL: Don't swear at me, I'm your friend

RYAN: [*genuine*] Sorry

Pause.

BILLY: What time is it now?

SAL: Nearly lockdown

RYAN: Back to our rooms

BILLY: My brother's getting married today

SAL: True?

BILLY: It might be happening soon. Really soon

SAL: I love weddings

BILLY: I was gonna be one of his—You know the guys that stand up the front?

SAL: I've always wanted to be one of them

BILLY: Same

SAL: Get to wear a nice suit …

BILLY: When they planned it, we thought I'd be out by now

SAL: … With a little flower

RYAN: Weddings are overrated

SAL: It's a day of love, family

BILLY: It's my big brother

SAL: And suits!

RYAN: It's everyone you know in one place, taking photos, pretending they talk to each other and getting fucked up. It's the same as funerals, you know there'll be a fight. We're not missing much out there, just all the reasons we got locked up in the first place

BILLY: It'll take more than a wedding for me to mess up again

SAL: That's why you need strategy when you leave

BILLY: Gym and chapel for you, hey

SAL: Gotta stay holy

RYAN: I don't need that

SAL: Keeps me on the path

BILLY: I dunno what I need. I just wanna get out

SAL: Don't think about the time or it takes even longer

BILLY: I think the wedding might be happening right now

Pause.

RYAN: When we're all released, we'll still, like, hang. Yeah?

SAL: Yeah

BILLY: Sure

Pause.

Might not work, though

SAL: How would we meet up?

RYAN: I'll message

SAL: You're from a different town

RYAN: So

BILLY: Eight hours away

RYAN: I'll drive

SAL: You don't have your license

RYAN: I'll get it

BILLY: Or a car

RYAN: Never stopped me

Another glance between BILLY *and* SAL.

What? We can't just never see each other ever again

BILLY: It doesn't matter yet, we've still got months

SAL: Years

BILLY: More free time

SAL: More KFC Fridays

SAL *and* BILLY *go back to passing the ball.*

RYAN: Fuck this. I'm gonna find that kid

SAL: Don't

RYAN: He flicked my cap. That's how it starts. If I don't show him the rules now, then, then—

SAL: You'll ruin your good behaviour

BILLY: And we won't get to stay up

RYAN: It's not like we'll be staying up much longer together anyway

SAL *and* BILLY *stop passing the ball.*

Something happened. The judge—He dropped my charges

BILLY: All of them?

RYAN: The heavy ones. My lawyer says I might get out next week

SAL: Next week!

RYAN: Mum says she'll buy me two motorbikes

BILLY: Two!

Pause.

Wow, that's, that's—

SAL: Soon
BILLY: How does that even happen?
RYAN: Dunno. Maybe it won't. Maybe it won't work out
SAL: You're so lucky, bro
RYAN: I don't want a motorbike. I don't even really wanna go home. Not yet
BILLY: But you get to leave
SAL: You get to be free
RYAN: Yeah, but then what?

No-one has an answer.

I'm gonna get a sick tattoo, though. Yeah, I'm gonna get my number tattooed, right … here. This place has always been good to me

SCENE 6: TRAIN STATION

ISAIAH *and* SHANIKA *wait at the train station.*

SHANIKA *eats McDonald's chips from a bag.* ISAIAH *nervously checks the arrival times.*

SHANIKA: I need my fries hot, salty. As salty as you can get
ISAIAH: Which train is it again?
SHANIKA: No KFC. None of that Hungry Jack's shit either
ISAIAH: Shanika, which train?
SHANIKA: Maccas chips are all I wanna eat.

She notices ISAIAH *is very nervous.*

What's wrong with you?
ISAIAH: I've gotta go
SHANIKA: What?
ISAIAH: Yeah, I forgot, I've got something on
SHANIKA: What thing? Where?
ISAIAH: None of your business
SHANIKA: Hang on
ISAIAH: Sorry

ISAIAH *goes to leave.* SHANIKA *blocks him.*

SHANIKA: Her train's here in a few minutes
ISAIAH: I have to be there now, like, I was already 'sposed to be there, it's—it's

SHANIKA: What?

ISAIAH: Work

SHANIKA: You told me you got work off because Mum's getting out today. You told me you'd come with me to get her from the train. You told me you'd wait until she got here

ISAIAH: I know, but he, um—he literally just texted me then, needs me to come in

SHANIKA: No, he didn't

ISAIAH: He did

SHANIKA: Show me

ISAIAH: I'm not showing you my phone

SHANIKA: I won't look at your dick pics, I just wanna see the text

ISAIAH: No

SHANIKA: Show me the message

ISAIAH: No

SHANIKA: Show me! Isaiah!

ISAIAH: I don't have to show you anything

SHANIKA: 'Cause you're lying! You don't have to be fucking anywhere!

Someone walks past and looks at them. SHANIKA *clocks it immediately.*

WHAT?

ISAIAH: Shanika

SHANIKA: [*continuing to call out to them*] WHAT YOU LOOKING AT?

SHANIKA *throws her bag of chips in the direction of the person.*

FUCK OFF!

ISAIAH: Shanika!

SHANIKA: Just go then, Isaiah, if you wanna leave so bad

I SEE YOU, YEAH KEEP GOING, KEEP WALKING, YEAH

ISAIAH: Stop it

He tries to pull her away. She resists.

SHANIKA: Get off me

ISAIAH: Do you always have to make everything hard?

SHANIKA: I did nothin wrong

ISAIAH: Can't take you anywhere. Can't even leave you alone

SHANIKA: I know how to look after myself

ISAIAH: That's why you call me up whenever you're in trouble?

SHANIKA: That was weeks ago, it was late, I had to

ISAIAH: And the week before that

SHANIKA: Aunty Kay couldn't come get me, she had that appointment and the cops had held me for ages

ISAIAH: And the time before

SHANIKA: Get over it

ISAIAH: I would if you didn't keep starting fights

SHANIKA: Me? That last one wasn't me, it was that bitch, Tahlia. You know what she said, I told you what she said to me, remember?

ISAIAH: Doesn't matter what she said

SHANIKA: Doesn't matter? Doesn't matter? She was talking shit about our mum, Isaiah. I don't care who it is, if anyone calls my mum a hairy slut I'm coming for them. I didn't even care that I was in thongs, I ran after her. Should've seen Tahlia's face. She was fucking scared

ISAIAH: Yeah, 'cause you smacked her

SHANIKA: A couple of times. Not hard or anything

ISAIAH: She was on the ground

SHANIKA: I don't even remember kicking her. Dunno where the cops got that part from

ISAIAH: It's in the video

SHANIKA: Well, I didn't know I was doing it, alright. I was blacked out or something, and I've never seen her since and she'll never say it again, so

ISAIAH: That's not the point

SHANIKA: You can't let people go round staring at you and saying shit about you, Isaiah. You let someone walk over you once, they'll just keep doing it. Then they'll see what else they can get away with, and then it gets worse, and it never, ever, ends

Pause.

Just go, go to work, go wherever the fuck you're going. I don't care. I'll tell Mum you said hello

ISAIAH *is conflicted. He really doesn't want to be here.*

ISAIAH: Nah. Promised I'd wait

He picks up SHANIKA*'s McDonald's. Inspects the chips. Gives them to her.*

Still salty

SHANIKA *goes back to eating again.*

It's just … been a while since—since I seen her, you know

SHANIKA: She'll be so happy today now she's out. And seeing us both here. Wonder which carriage she'll be in. I wanna be standing right there when the doors open

ISAIAH: Shanika

SHANIKA: It's gonna be different now. She's gonna live with us at Aunty Kay's and we're all gonna be together and it'll be better, like a—like a family again

ISAIAH: I dunno

SHANIKA: It won't be like, when we were living with

ISAIAH: Stockie

SHANIKA: Yeah, him. It's not gonna be like that anymore

ISAIAH: Depends how long she lasts this time

SHANIKA: She's not going back. She's home for good. Stockie was the reason she got locked up and he's gone now, so

ISAIAH: Who told you that

SHANIKA: Aunty Kay

ISAIAH *shakes his head.*

Yeah, Mum didn't, she didn't realise the—there was this whole thing, they were together, but he didn't—Stockie didn't tell Mum all the gear was

ISAIAH: She knew

SHANIKA: No she didn't

ISAIAH: Yes she did

SHANIKA: How would you know, you were what—twelve?

ISAIAH: You're younger than me

SHANIKA: Yeah but Aunty Kay told me the truth, alright

ISAIAH: Aunty Kay wasn't there

SHANIKA: She still knows what happened, she was at the courts

ISAIAH: Exactly

SHANIKA: So she knows it wasn't Mum's fault

ISAIAH: Maybe she didn't mean to but she can't help it, she's just—she's a shit mum

SHANIKA: Don't you dare say that about my mum

ISAIAH: I can say what I want, she's my mum too

SHANIKA: She's not a shit mum, she—why would she wanna be locked up, huh? She didn't wanna be taken away from us, not again, she didn't know she was gonna be taken

ISAIAH: She was part of the whole thing with Stockie

SHANIKA: You don't know what the fuck you're talking about

ISAIAH: Yes, I do

SHANIKA: You're a fucking idiot, Isaiah, a fucking idiot

ISAIAH: Shut the hell up

SHANIKA: No, you shut up, you're an idiot, you've been listening to people

ISAIAH: What people?

SHANIKA: I dunno, people, people at your new job

ISAIAH: My job?

SHANIKA: Thinking you're so flash now or whatever

ISAIAH: Oh fuck off

SHANIKA: You can be all flash but you still don't know anything 'cause I'm telling you now it was Stockie's fault she got locked up and Stockie's fault she went away, because Stockie was the one who made her do it

ISAIAH: They made me

Pause.

SHANIKA: Made you what?

ISAIAH: Nothing

SHANIKA: No, what?

ISAIAH: I said nothing

SHANIKA: You're the one who brought it up

ISAIAH: Keep believing what you want. You'll like it better this way

SHANIKA *glares at* ISAIAH.

She prods him.

Don't

SHANIKA: You gonna tell me?

She prods him harder.

You gonna tell me now?

ISAIAH: Stop it

SHANIKA: Tell me Isaiah

ISAIAH: No

She shoves him.

Shanika!

SHANIKA: I wanna know

Pause.

ISAIAH: They took me everywhere

SHANIKA: Who? Where?

ISAIAH: People's houses … They made me carry the stuff for them

Pause.

SHANIKA: You were working for Stockie?

ISAIAH: Not like I was getting paid

SHANIKA: Fucking Stockie. That would've been—that would've been so his idea, I hate him, I hate him!

ISAIAH: No, it was Mum. 'Do whatever Stockie says, he's gonna help us, we need him'

SHANIKA: Why would she say that? We didn't need him

ISAIAH: I guess we did

SHANIKA: But I—I never saw this, never heard anything

ISAIAH: You were little. And I'd only just started high school. And Mum said don't tell anyone and … and so I didn't, I … . I just did whatever they said, 'cause … 'Cause, I dunno. I didn't know what else to do

Pause.

But I'm doing pretty good now, I'm

SHANIKA: Nah, this is all bullshit

ISAIAH: It's not much, but I'm getting my own money with this job and

SHANIKA: Bullshit. Just bullshit

ISAIAH: I've been thinking how I could have my own place one day, maybe one day have my own business too, be my own boss

SHANIKA: Doing what?

ISAIAH: It doesn't matter

SHANIKA: Well, it does, you can't just be your own boss doing nothing

ISAIAH: It won't be nothing, it'll be something and I'm not talking about now, I'm talking about one day

SHANIKA: What does this have to do with Mum?

ISAIAH: I don't really wanna see her

SHANIKA: You have to

ISAIAH: I know how it'll go

SHANIKA: It'll be different this time

ISAIAH *doesn't reply.*

Wait, are you serious? Isaiah, it's Mum. Our mum. She loves you, she's been locked up all this time, missing us. What happened with Stockie—You gotta give her another chance

ISAIAH: I'm gonna go live with some mates from work

SHANIKA: What?

ISAIAH: This is why I didn't wanna come to the train

SHANIKA: You're moving out?

ISAIAH: Somewhere close. I just wanna work, you know … Stable income, money to have fun with my life, do something. You know what it's like with her—no matter what, something always happens and—and it's gonna be me who has to fix it and it'll just ruin everything I've been working on and …

He looks at SHANIKA. *She has melted completely.*

Shanika?

She turns away from him.

Sis?

She won't let him see her face.

I just wanna start fresh

Pause.

SHANIKA: Don't leave me, Isaiah

ISAIAH: I'm not

SHANIKA: Please don't leave me

ISAIAH: I'm not leaving you, I just don't wanna live with her

SHANIKA: But if you're not living with her that means you're not with me. It was meant to be us three together. Us three together at Aunty Kay's, before—before everything changes again

ISAIAH: This change could be good

SHANIKA: Good for you. But what about me? What am I 'sposed to do? I'm not ready. I don't know how to be a mum

Pause.

ISAIAH: What?

SHANIKA: Aunty Kay said she'd help—taking care of it, with school and everything. And Mum will be back. But you. You're the only one who makes me feel better, Isaiah. The only one

ISAIAH *doesn't know what to do.*

The train pulls into the station. They turn to greet their mum.

SCENE 7: PHOTOGRAPHY

JADE *is about to take a photograph. She's unsure about using the camera on her new subject.*

JADE: So, um, I think maybe if you stand … there.
Or maybe you should sit. Yeah, sit.
And I'll stand here, so I can take the photo from this angle …
Oh, but then the light's wrong.
Sorry, Ms Mosely lent me this. I'm still getting the hang of it …

She fumbles with the settings.

It's flash, hey. Bit too flash for me. I used to take photos on my phone, but lately Ms Mosely got me using this proper camera. She says I have 'the essence' and that she wants to see whatever I can see.

I don't see anything special.

Oh, no offence.

I just mean, anything I see, someone's probably already seen it and taken a photo. And what is 'the essence', anyway?

Ms Mosley said don't worry about any of that and let inspiration strike. This was after the second—no, I think it was the third … Yeah, the third time I got locked up. I was in for a week and none of us ate the food 'cause it was gross, and some kids flooded the whole precinct, and it was getting serious, like they were saying I could be in there even longer next time. So when I got out, Ms Mosley said, we need to keep you in school and out of trouble, Miss Jade. I said, good luck!

Sorry, this won't take much longer.

Looks through the eyepiece. Something is wrong. She panics.

Aw, what?! It's gone all dark. Is it broken? I think it's broken. Shit! I've broken it already!

She inspects the camera again.

Oh.

She takes off the cap, embarrassed.

I have taken photos before, it's just—those other times I wasn't trying very hard.

Actually, I didn't even do anything with the camera at first. I kept forgetting I had it.

Then one day at school, Ms Mosley asked how my photos were going. She wasn't happy when I said I hadn't taken any, not happy at all. I don't like upsetting Ms Mosley. She's so nice all the time.

So I took the camera to school the next day. I kept thinking about it in my bag, but I never took it out 'cause, I dunno, I felt weird walking around with it, with people looking at me, thinking that I think I'm some kind of photographer or something when I really don't.

But I didn't want to disappoint Ms Mosley again. So when I got to the city, I finally took it out. No-one even noticed. I walked around and around. I took photos of buildings, trees, someone's dog … but I hated them. Dunno why. Just hated them.

I got to the food court in the city where I meet my friends and I was sitting there kinda, kinda sad I guess—'cause I didn't have anything to take a photo of. Then I noticed how my friend Blake always sits with his arms crossed, like this, and how Molly always takes her hair in and out her ponytail, like she can never decide if she wants it up or down, and Sarah looks so serious when she's eating so you don't touch her food—like, seriously, don't touch Sarah's nuggets or you'll die.

I thought maybe they'd think it was weird, but they really liked it, loved it, me taking photos of them. But I had to say, act natural, it's not about the posing it's about … it's about 'the essence'!

I didn't even stay out late, I went home early that afternoon to look through all the photos I took. They were kinda good, I mean, I liked them, but I thought this can't be it, this can't be what Ms Mosely meant.

I sent them to my friends, but I told Ms Mosely I didn't take any.

Guess I should take your photo for real now.

She holds the camera up landscape to take a photo. She doesn't like it.

No, not that.

She turns the camera portrait. She still doesn't like it.

That's not it.

She crouches down and changes the angle. It's still not right.

Ugh, I swear I was getting it good the other time.

She fumbles with the camera settings again.

So, then, Sarah, she was looking at the photos I took of everyone on her phone, and Ms Mosley saw them. And then Ms Mosley came up to me, and said she loved them, said she wanted me to take more, for me to take pictures of everyone in school!

She tries to set up the photo one more time.

I can't get it. I'm not getting it!

She gives up and puts the camera down.

This is why I said no when she asked me. I knew I couldn't take photos of people, I don't see anything different and I don't have the essence, I never had the essence and it's a shit camera anyway!

I left it on her desk and I didn't talk to her, didn't go to school for a week. It was a waste of time, and I didn't need it.

But then I was in the city again and I was walking around like I always do and it didn't feel the same. I kept seeing things, seeing people, my friends, their faces, those funny times when they think I'm not looking and …

Kinda like that. What you're doing now.

She picks the camera back up.

Click.

Hmmm …

Click.

Anyway, my friend Molly keeps asking me if I want a photo, but oh no, I prefer to stay behind the camera, in control of the photo, thank you.

Click.

And I'm kinda in it already anyway, 'cause it's like, the essence of the photo is me, seeing you.

She flicks through the photos she has just taken.

Oh, I like these. A few more. Keep doing what you're doing. Just be yourself!

Click, click, click.

SCENE 8: BIRTHDAY CAKE

JARRAH *and* ASH *run inside the house. They check out the window to see if they are still being followed.*

JARRAH: Still there?
ASH: Don't think so
JARRAH: Maybe they weren't following us. Maybe it wasn't even them
ASH: They must've left

They exhale.

ASH *shoves* JARRAH.

Why'd you start that for?
JARRAH: It wasn't just me
ASH: Was I 'sposed to stand there and watch? We should've let him go
JARRAH: It's not like anyone from the '05[1] wouldn't do the same thing if they saw us out alone. It was the only way to get back at them for Darius

1. The gang name '05 is based on their postcode, and should be pronounced 'Oh-Five'.

ASH: Darius started it up with them first

JARRAH: No, he only smashed those windows *after* they jumped him

ASH: Yeah, and look how that all turned out. Now we don't even know where he is

JARRAH: Coward

ASH: He had to hide. They're looking for him everywhere. And now they'll be looking for us

ASH *checks out the window again.*

JARRAH: It's alright. We'll lay low, stay round home for a bit

ASH: You heard what they did to Joey right

JARRAH: Joey was dumb. He was on their side of Cres Road

ASH: Nah dude, they got Joey outside his house

JARRAH: What?

ASH: Six of them. They don't care about Cres Road anymore. That's why I've got my knife, for protection

JARRAH: Could you really use it?

ASH: If I had to

JARRAH: What about the Park Line?

ASH: I've seen them there. And outside the BP

JARRAH: Fuck

ASH: They don't care about the rules anymore. I hate them. I hate them so much, I wish they'd—

JARRAH: They can't die. They're roaches

A heaviness between them about what they've just done.

ASH: Maybe we went too hard

JARRAH: He was okay

ASH: Was he?

JARRAH: I think

ASH: If he's okay then he's told his crew by now. They won't be far off

JARRAH: Not while my uncle's home. They never mess with him

NIKKI *enters with a birthday cake.*

NIKKI: Happy birthday, Jarrah!

ASH: It's your birthday?

NIKKI: Sixteen, right? Sixteen?

JARRAH: Fifteen

ASH: I didn't know it was your birthday

NIKKI: I remembered it's around when the Christmas decorations come out in the shops

ASH: You never said it was your birthday

JARRAH: Where's my mum at?

NIKKI: The couch

JARRAH *is disappointed.*

JARRAH: She said we were gonna—Oh well. Uncle's here. We'll have cake with Uncle then

NIKKI: Nah, he just left

A look between JARRAH *and* ASH.

ASH: Left?

JARRAH: What do you mean, he left?

NIKKI: He went out

JARRAH: Where?

ASH: Is he coming back?

NIKKI *knows something she isn't telling them.*

NIKKI: Dunno. He left kinda quickly

ASH *looks out the window again.*

JARRAH: I'll call him

He gets out his phone but NIKKI *interrupts.*

NIKKI: So … cuz … you liked the cake, right? I got chocolate 'cause I know you like chocolate

Pause.

Do you have any change?

JARRAH: You're asking me for money? It's my birthday

NIKKI: So?

JARRAH: Did you get me a present?

NIKKI: I got you a cake

JARRAH: Did you pay for it?

NIKKI: No

JARRAH: Why would I give you money if you didn't get me a present?

NIKKI: Well I didn't get you a present 'cause I don't have any money

JARRAH: Well we've got a cake so what do you want money for now?

NIKKI *doesn't reply.*

No, Nikki

NIKKI: Please, I really need it

JARRAH *makes the call. He waits for Uncle to pick up.*

Look at me, Jarrah, look. Look! My eyelashes are non-existent. See these eyelids? See? Basically bald

Uncle doesn't answer the phone.

ASH: Did he answer?

JARRAH: No

NIKKI: I just really need my lashes done. It's not that expensive

JARRAH: I'm not paying for that shit

NIKKI: But I'm so ugly right now. Fresh lashes could be like—like my birthday gift to you

ASH: Try him again

JARRAH *calls again.*

NIKKI: Well then, can I have money for my phone? Your mum said she'd give me some but then she forgot, and I can't find her purse

JARRAH: Why isn't he answering?

NIKKI: He's probably like me, I can't even receive calls anymore. My account is suspended. That's how bad it is. I'm fully uncontactable

Uncle still doesn't pick up.

ASH: What do we do?

JARRAH: Wait, I guess. He doesn't usually go anywhere long

ASH: I don't like this

JARRAH: What do you want me to do?

NIKKI: So if not for my phone, what about money for food?

JARRAH: Stop it, Nikki. I'm not giving you anything

NIKKI *turns to* ASH.

NIKKI: Do you have twenty dollars? I'll pay you back

JARRAH: She won't

NIKKI: If Ash wants to give me a loan, he can

ASH: I don't have twenty dollars, sorry

NIKKI: How 'bout ten?

JARRAH: Don't give it to her

NIKKI: Jarrah!

JARRAH: I got told not to give you any money

NIKKI: By who?

JARRAH: Mum

NIKKI: What?! But she said

JARRAH: This is some classic Nikki shit

NIKKI: I knew you were all against me

JARRAH: No-one's against you

NIKKI: Yeah, you, your mum, my mum, Uncle, Nana. The whole world

JARRAH: You were trying to bribe me with a stolen birthday cake

NIKKI: I still remembered your birthday, though. No-one else is here, are they?

JARRAH: [*to* ASH] We're not giving her money 'cause she keeps running away

NIKKI: Money or no money, if I ever wanna leave somewhere, I'll leave

JARRAH: Then Mum gets the cops calling from the hospital to come pick her up and—

NIKKI: She got that call? I thought—Why didn't anyone get me?

JARRAH: She couldn't drive. And you were three hours away. And it was two a.m.

NIKKI: There was nowhere to sleep. They made me stay at the hospital until the morning and no-one there believed me. The nurses thought I was making it up and I wasn't, I wasn't making it up

ASH: Three hours? Why do you go so far?

NIKKI: 'Cause

JARRAH: You should just stay here, with us

NIKKI: I am. I will. That's not what the money is for

JARRAH: Then what is it?

NIKKI: Oh, come on, Jarrah, please

JARRAH: Nup

NIKKI: Don't bother then

JARRAH: I wasn't giving it to you anyway

NIKKI: But why not? Why is everyone like this to me? Everyone else gets to buy stuff and go wherever they want. I wanna live too

JARRAH *doesn't budge.*

Fine. I'm eating cake

NIKKI *starts eating the birthday cake.*

ASH*'s fears are starting to get the better of him.*

ASH: What if it's like what happened with Joey? What if they come back with more people, wait for us in the dark, behind fences, corners

JARRAH: They won't

ASH: How do you know?

JARRAH: I don't

ASH: And if not tonight, it'll be tomorrow, and if not tomorrow, the night after that. We can't go anywhere now

JARRAH: Can you chill for a second?

ASH: How? How can I chill when it's gonna be like this forever and I didn't even wanna fight that kid. I don't wanna be like Darius

JARRAH: We've gotta be like Uncle, that's why. It took him years, but if you keep fighting back, they'll leave you alone

ASH: I can't be like Uncle

JARRAH: You were like Uncle tonight

ASH: I wanna be normal

JARRAH: This is normal

ASH: No, live, like—Like what she was saying

NIKKI: Why do you all hate them so much? The '05

ASH *and* JARRAH *look at each other then back to* NIKKI*, genuinely stumped.*

JARRAH: I dunno, it's just—it's the way it is?

ASH: It's how it's always been with the postcodes

JARRAH: Even before us

Pause.

NIKKI: So, Darius is hiding from the '05 now

JARRAH: He's hiding from everyone, really

NIKKI: And you don't know where he is, not even a little bit

ASH: No-one does. That's the point

JARRAH: Hope he's alright

Pause.

NIKKI: If you'd been nicer to me, maybe gave me some money for eyelashes or phone credit or a train ticket then maybe I could've told you where Darius is

ASH: You know where he went?
JARRAH: She's lying. She does this
NIKKI: I'm not lying! Why does everyone always say I'm lying!
JARRAH: 'Cause you lie all the time
NIKKI: So do you. So does everyone
ASH: Where is he then? How come you know and we don't?
NIKKI: 'Cause he was here before. With Uncle. He's been taking care of him, making sure he's always got places to sleep. But I dunno, something happened and they had to leave
ASH: Do you know where they went?
NIKKI: I know I need twenty dollars
JARRAH: This isn't funny
NIKKI: I know right, it's actually not funny at all
ASH: Just give her the money
JARRAH: No, tell us Nikki
NIKKI: How is that fair?
JARRAH: 'Cause this is serious. We need Uncle's help
ASH: And we need to see Darius
NIKKI: And I need to see my boyfriend
JARRAH: What boyfriend?
NIKKI: He's like so much more mature than you and all the boys. He loves me, and he has a business and everything
JARRAH: He sounds old
NIKKI: Twenty-six isn't old
JARRAH: Yeah it is
ASH: I don't care who her boyfriend is
JARRAH: So that's why you keep running away
NIKKI: I promise I'll come back, I just need to visit him tonight, okay
ASH: Just give her the money
JARRAH: But she doesn't know anything! She just wants attention

NIKKI*'s phone rings.*

She quickly turns it off, but JARRAH *clocked it.*

Thought you couldn't get calls
NIKKI: Fine, I won't see my boyfriend and you won't see Darius and we can all just eat cake. Happy birthday!

JARRAH *grabs* NIKKI.

JARRAH: Tell me Nikki, you slut

NIKKI: Don't call me that!

ASH: Stop it, Jarrah!

JARRAH: No! Not until she tells us

JARRAH *won't let* NIKKI *go, so* ASH *reaches into* JARRAH*'s pockets, searching for money.*

What're you doing?

ASH: I'm over this

JARRAH: Don't touch me

ASH: It's twenty bucks, who cares

JARRAH *lets go of* NIKKI *and turns on* ASH.

JARRAH: I do

NIKKI: Jarrah, don't!

JARRAH *and* ASH *start wrestling.*

Leave him alone!

JARRAH *is getting particularly intense.* ASH *pulls out his knife.* JARRAH *takes a step back.*

JARRAH: Whoa

NIKKI: Oh my god

ASH: I don't wanna use it, but he's, he's

NIKKI: Then put it down

JARRAH: What you gonna do, Ash?

ASH: Don't be an idiot

JARRAH: You're not gonna use that on me

ASH: I could

JARRAH: Yeah?

ASH: Yeah!

It looks like they are about to fight for real, but then DARIUS *barges into the house, out of breath.*

DARIUS: Uncle? You here? Uncle!

ASH: Darius?!

DARIUS *sees them all standing there with the knife.*

DARIUS: What the hell?

JARRAH and ASH rush over to him, their fight completely forgotten.

JARRAH: Where you been, brother?

DARIUS: Is Uncle home? Did he come back?

JARRAH: We thought he was with you

DARIUS: He dropped me at the Cameron house to sleep tonight, but then—they found me

ASH: What? How?

DARIUS: Someone must've seen me or tipped them off. They rocked up at the house, but I bolted

JARRAH: Lucky you got away

DARIUS: Nah, I was running here along Cres Road and even more of them saw me

ASH: Cres Road!

NIKKI: Wait—now the '05 know where you are?

JARRAH: Here? With us?

DARIUS: I'm sorry, I wasn't thinking. I just thought Uncle would be home

ASH: Fuck!

JARRAH: We have to go

NIKKI: What?

JARRAH: None of us can be here right now

NIKKI: What about my money?

ASH: Doesn't matter

NIKKI: But I need to see my boyfriend

JARRAH: Stick with us. He's bad for you

DARIUS: We have to leave before they find us

JARRAH: We'll take the back way. Let's find Uncle together

They are rushing out when DARIUS notices the birthday cake.

DARIUS: [*sincere*] Oh, happy birthday

JARRAH: Come on!

The boys race out of the house. NIKKI quickly follows behind.

SCENE 9: BAIL BED

CORBAN *has just arrived at his aunty's front door. They haven't spoken in months.*

CORBAN: Hey, Aunt.

No, wait, wait!

It's only me. No-one else. I'm by myself, see?

Sorry, I didn't mean to—This isn't—I know you don't really like me at the moment but … I was just wondering if maybe, um, could I maybe stay here tonight? Please? I can sleep outside if you want, if that makes you feel better, I don't mind. Anywhere is fine really, 'cause um—

Well, so you know my mate, Frankie? Yeah, Frankie. You like Frankie. So I been staying at his the past week but, um, his parents just came home, and they said they'd be another few days but they literally just rocked up, like, completely unexpected. I know it's their own house to rock up to whenever they want but still, they said, they told Frankie they'd be back later after the weekend and it's only Friday and—and we hadn't even cleaned up yet, like we were fully gonna clean up—Oh no, it wasn't anything bad, we didn't have a party, no, no parties or anything, it was just like, I dunno what all the mess was. I guess I'm just not that good at making the bed.

Anyway, all the mess kind of made them realise I was living in their house while they were away and they didn't really want me staying there anymore, which is fair, I guess. I didn't wanna make things hard for Frankie so I said that's all sweet man, I've got somewhere else to go.

Except … well, except I lied 'cause I kinda don't. I wasn't expecting to have to find somewhere else today, like not at such short notice and everything, and it's bad timing as well because um, well there's a couple of reasons why it's bad timing.

This is gonna sound bad, but just so you know, Kara says I've really turned a leaf. I've been going to the centre heaps and to all my sessions with her and that's why today I decided I'm gonna do the right thing, I'm gonna turn myself in for, for— just something that happened last week.

So yeah, I talked to Kara about turning myself in 'cause I just kinda wanna be clean-slate about it, you know. But by the time I decided that, it was already past three, and Kara always says, if you're gonna go, go first thing in the morning 'cause it takes all day—first to the cops, then to the courts, to see if you'll get bail or not. And since you can also only get processed during business hours, like banks and stuff, if you hand yourself in too late, they put you off till the next day 'cause they all have to finish work. So then you have to stay there overnight. And today being Friday is the worst. If I went in after three, on a Friday, I'd have to be in lock-up till Monday. Fuck that! Oh, sorry. But seriously, I'm not gonna turn myself in today just so they could put me in jail the whole weekend. For real. Who would do that? No-one.

So I promised Kara I'd turn myself in first thing Monday instead and she said she'd come with me. But after this whole thing with Frankie's house … I dunno anymore. It was fine before, when I had Frankie's place to stay but now—Now I've got nowhere to get bailed to.

I've tried talking to Mum, Kara's tried, but she— she doesn't wanna see me since Dad got released and I don't wanna live with them anyway. Every time he sees me he says he still reckons I'm not his kid—but everyone else says we're two of the same, even though I try to be nothing like him. But I guess, yeah, sometimes, maybe I am a little bit.

Anyway, the thing is, if I go in on Monday I'm gonna need somewhere to get bailed to, 'cause last time—I don't know if you know about last time, how I didn't have an address? They didn't know where to put me and they were trying to find someplace for me to go but everywhere was full, or it was too late—it was like every place they thought of or called, there was nothing available. Nothing. And Kara was freaking out as well 'cause she'd been with me all day and she needed to go home to her family and I get that. In the end they did find somewhere, but it was um … Like it was fine and everything, but Kara didn't really want me to stay in an adult hostel when I'm only fourteen. Like she felt really bad leaving me there, but I said, it's okay, I'll be okay. It was the only bed they had left and the door to my room didn't really close properly, and I felt kinda weird 'cause some older guys were looking at me funny, so … So I didn't really sleep, just in case. But I was alright. Sharing a hostel room with a random old man is way better than being in lock-up. I think.

But still. I don't really wanna have to go there again either, especially not now, when I'm trying to be better.

Like I've already been making good choices for a while now, Aunt. Except for last week, but if you don't count that—I even stopped vaping. Yeah. 'Cause I realised they don't even know the long-term effects. Everyone I know is vaping and they have no idea what it's doing to them. I decided it's not worth it, if it's gonna hurt me later. And I don't do any drugs either. At all. Seriously, no drugs, just cones, and I've been staying away from—well, I'm not friends anymore with those people. You know, those ones I brought to your house, that time.

I don't know why I did that. Especially while you were at sorry business. I don't know why I let them in, or helped them steal from you, and break all your things. I just—I don't know why it happened.

But I know it was wrong and … and if you let me stay tonight then, then maybe I can still turn the leaf?

SCENE 10: COMMUNITY GARDEN

Two years have passed since Scene 1.

JONTY *is working in the garden at a regional youth centre.*

He plays music off his phone —something with a good beat. He sings along as he works.

He's giving himself over to the music when he spins around and finds KAI *staring at him.*

JONTY: Shit!

He drops his shovel.

KAI: Hey
JONTY: Kai—uh …

He tries to stop the music, but fumbles. He can't get it to stop.

He finally recovers and turns the music off.

When—when did you get back?

KAI: Yesterday

JONTY: I didn't hear

Pause.

How are you?

KAI: Glad to be home

JONTY: Yeah?

KAI: Yeah

JONTY *warily approaches* KAI.

They go to hug, but don't.

KAI *awkwardly plays with* JONTY*'s stubble instead.*

What's this?

JONTY: A beard

JONTY *tries to shrug him off.*

KAI: You call that a beard? Bro. That's two hairs. Three!

JONTY *continues to resist.*

Got some pubes now too?

JONTY: Kai!

He moves away.

KAI: You'll get there. Few more years maybe

JONTY: Least I don't have that haircut

KAI: Nah, this is a look, bro, it's a look

JONTY: Looks pretty shit

KAI: I'm glad you still know it's me. All this time, I thought you might've forgot

Pause.

So … what's got you in a good mood?

JONTY: I'm not—really

KAI: Oh yeah?

He sings a line from the song playing.

JONTY: It's a good song, alright

KAI: Yeah, it's a good song. Not your usual thing, though

JONTY: I've always liked this music

KAI: Since when?

JONTY: Since—I dunno. Been listening to some new stuff. Trynna branch out

KAI: Like when me and you were gonna start a band?

JONTY: Not a band. A duo

KAI: We were gonna write our own songs, make money, get famous. We were gonna show people we're making music out here. Real music

Pause.

All talk, hey. Probably wouldn't've worked out. Into plants now, I see?

JONTY: I'm just helping Vinny around the centre. We've started putting these new gardens in. Bush tucker

KAI: Nice

JONTY: Yeah

KAI: I came by 'cause Vinny says there's a bike in the back room I can use. My legs, man! Not used to all this walking. He says the bike's mine if I get it fixed up—I don't care if it works or not. I'm just happy to be out

JONTY: I didn't think you were coming back to town, after

KAI: That right?

JONTY: I mean, someone said—I thought you'd stay with your mum for a while

KAI: I'm living with my cousin. The Reserve is our home, Jonty. Since we were babies

JONTY: Yeah, I never wanna leave

KAI: Imagine leaving with chains on. Being driven hours away and locked in a box for a year

Pause.

JONTY: So you going back to school or

KAI: Nah they won't take me

JONTY: Why not?

KAI: Too much trouble. Too many offences

JONTY: But you did your time

KAI: You know how they've got new teachers out here every couple of months. They don't know me, they just took one look at my file and

JONTY: What are you s'posed to do?

KAI: What's this?

KAI starts picking up JONTY's gardening tools and playing with them. JONTY feels uncomfortable with the proximity. KAI doesn't put anything back in the right place.

JONTY: A shovel?

KAI: What about this one?

JONTY: Hedge … trimmers

KAI: And this?

JONTY: What does Vinny say?

KAI: Dunno

JONTY: He can talk to the school for you

KAI: He's helping me with the whole NDIS thing

JONTY: But what about school?

KAI: They reckon I should do Distance Ed

JONTY: That's alright then

KAI: Fuck Distance Ed. I'm not sitting inside all day. Been cooped up enough

JONTY: I guess if you moved towns, to your mum's

KAI: I'm not leaving home again

JONTY: But there'd be more schools there than here. They might take you

KAI: I don't need school, I'll get a job. I'll be working on the road as a lollipop man

JONTY: Really? They make good money

KAI: Yeah, I'll get the latest phone and everything

JONTY: That's sick. When do you start?

KAI: None of those jobs are going at the moment, but when there is

Pause.

JONTY: You only just got out, there's time

KAI: You sound like Vinny

JONTY: I like Vinny

KAI: Yeah, he's nice

JONTY: He's got me working at the centre once a week. I'm even going to school most days

KAI: Look at you
JONTY: Shut up
KAI: Being a good boy now
JONTY: I guess

Pause.

Vinny has been taking all the boys on these camping weekends with Uncle Max

KAI: [*not cool*] Cool

JONTY: I thought it sounded kinda lame too, but Vinny—you know how he is—talked me round. Called me up every day that week to remind me, drove to my house, picked me up in the bus. He wouldn't let off—I didn't have a choice, I just had to get in. So then we drove out to the Rocks

KAI: There's nothing to do at the Rocks

JONTY: Yeah there is. We went fishing, looked at the stars. Talked about mob. Uncle Max tells some pretty good stories. I think it helped

KAI: Helped how?

JONTY: I dunno— made me think about stuff, like … Like how I don't wanna do crime anymore

Pause.

KAI: And you didn't even need to get locked up
JONTY: Got pretty close

KAI: That's right. You were the only other person there that night, and every other night, we did everything together, but it all worked out for you

JONTY: Kai
KAI: I thought we were brothers
JONTY: We are
KAI: Brothers don't snitch
JONTY: It wasn't like that
KAI: I had your back, you were s'posed to have mine
JONTY: They brought me in, they knew something already

KAI: You say 'no interview'. You gave them a chance to ask you questions, to get it out of you

JONTY: They already knew it was us who'd done the break and enters. And all those fires

KAI: They didn't know anything for sure, they just tell you that. Why'd you fall for it?

JONTY: I dunno

KAI: What did they say?

JONTY: I don't remember, they were saying lots of stuff, it was confusing

KAI: So confusing you snitched?

JONTY: Something about good behaviour, work with Vinny, stay out of prison

KAI: There it is

JONTY: I didn't know it meant you were gonna get locked up. I thought I'd saved the both of us, but it was too late, there was nothing I could do

KAI: You could've visited me. Or called. I sat there waiting

JONTY: I felt too shit. I still feel shit

KAI: You seem fine to me. Out here singing, gardening, off on your camping trips with Uncle Max, telling me you don't wanna do crime no more, when I went to jail and it was all because of you

JONTY: I know, I'm—I'm sorry, Kai

Pause.

KAI: It's done now

JONTY: I wish I could take it back—but I dunno how

KAI: I just know I don't wanna go away ever again. I wanna stay here, always

JONTY: Good, 'cause it wasn't the same without you

KAI: Oh yeah?

JONTY: Nah

KAI: Thought so

Pause.

So, what you doing now?

JONTY: Nothing really

KAI: We could go to the creek

JONTY: Or the servo. Get lollies?

KAI: I guess there'll be some trucks coming through?

JONTY: What about camping? I think we're going again this weekend. Wanna come?

KAI: Maybe

JONTY: I'll play good music
KAI: Why? You wanna hear me sing again?
JONTY: Yeah, maybe
KAI: Only if you give me a good beat
JONTY: Deal
KAI: Deal

They do their special handshake.

Love you, brother
JONTY: Love you.

THE END

About the ATYP Juvenile Justice Progam

Australian Theatre for Young People (ATYP) works in partnership with the NSW Government, Department of Communities and Justice, and with generous support from the Neilson Foundation, to deliver theatre workshops in every Youth Justice Centre across New South Wales.

Titled *The Arts as a Driver of Positive Change*, this two-hour workshop builds confidence and communication skills through performance. Using scenes from *Saplings* by Hannah Belanszky, an award-winning play about young people in conflict with the law and the justice system, professional ATYP artists perform live excerpts, invite participants to direct emotional changes, and even step into the scene themselves. The session concludes with an open discussion about creative expression and pathways into the Arts.

Through these workshops, young people in detention engage with stories that mirror their own experiences, discovering new ways to express themselves and imagine different futures. The program embodies ATYP's belief that creativity can be a catalyst for transformation, ensuring that every young person, regardless of their circumstances, is seen, heard, and valued.

About ATYP

ATYP exists to create theatre by and for young people, championing their stories, perspectives, and potential. Through performance, workshops, and school programs, we empower the next generation of storytellers and audiences, igniting the creative spirit of young Australians, providing them with the tools to enrich Australia's cultural life with their stories.

Our Staff

ARTISTIC DIRECTOR & CEO
Hayden Tonazzi

CREATIVE PRODUCER & ASSOCIATE ARTIST
Ryan Whitworth-Jones

EDUCATION MANAGER & RESIDENT ARTIST
George Kemp

WORKSHOPS MANAGER
Kate Murphy

RESIDENT DRAMATURG
Jane FitzGerald

VENUE MANAGER
Tom Hughes

PROGRAMS & DEVELOPMENT OFFICER
Alex Fry

MARKETING OFFICER
Melanie Raveendran

ARCHIVIST
Judith Seeff